OPEN ROAD

30 Days of Creative Prayer for People Who Are Too Busy to Pray

TIM MORRAL

MELISSA McDONALD MORRAL

Granola Soul

Rochester, NY

Copyright © 2015 Timothy Morral/Melissa McDonald Morral
All rights reserved.

ISBN 978-0-692-56580-3

Unless otherwise indicated, all Scripture citations are taken from the *New Revised Standard Version Bible*, copyright 1989, Division of Christian Education of the National Council of the Churches of Christ in the United States of America. Used by permission. All rights reserved.

To Caity and Meg, always.

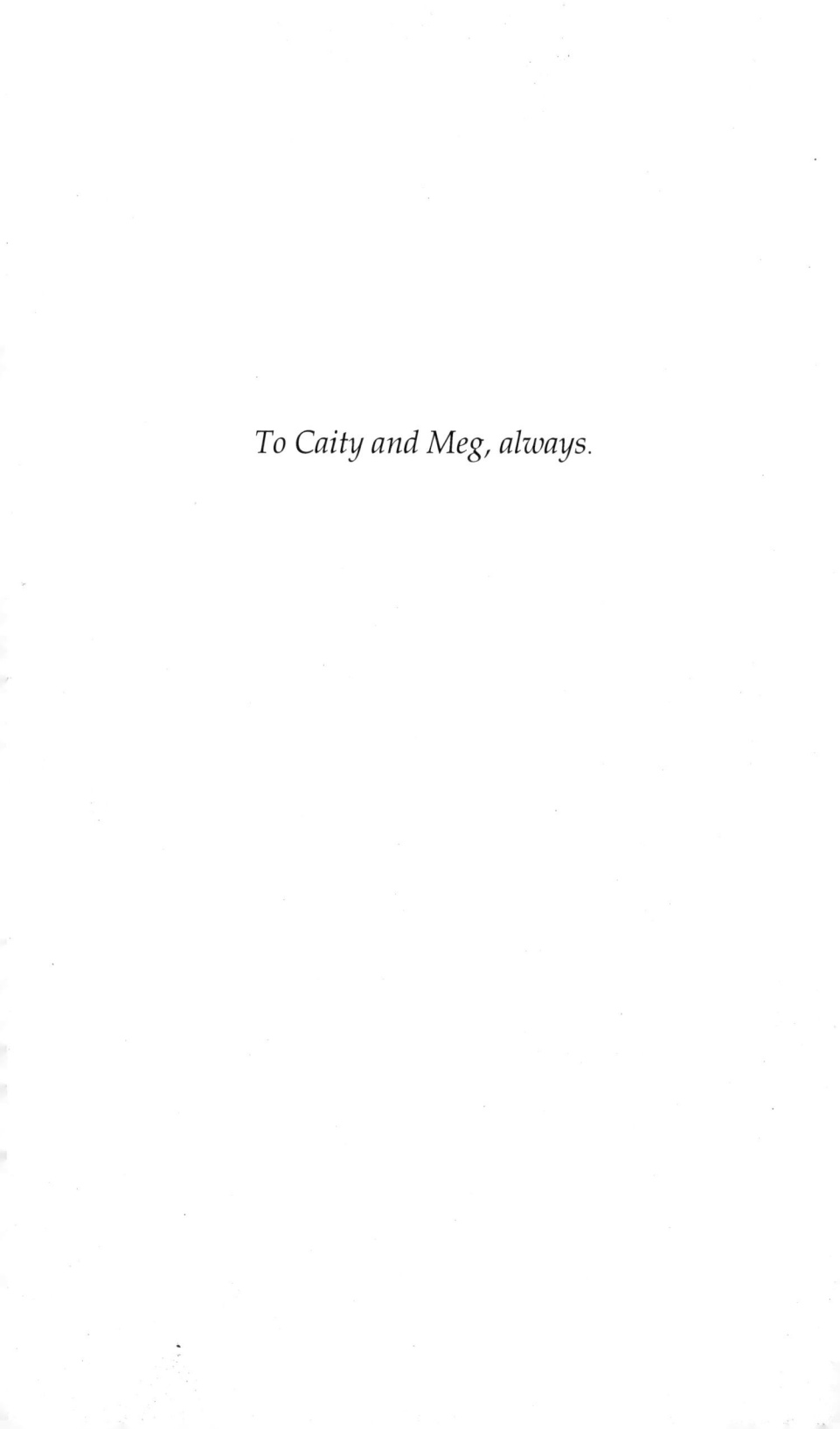

CONTENTS

	Acknowledgments	i
1	Introduction	1
2	How to Use This Book	7
3	Ground Rules for Prayer	11

PART I

4	A Road Map: Making Room for God	17
5	On the Road: Starting Conversations	29
6	Gaining Speed: Using Intuition	43
7	Home: Finding Joy in God's Presence	55

PART II

Day 1: The Mustard Seed 67

Day 2: Seeds + Soil 69

Day 3: A Lost Son 72

Day 4: A Storm at Sea 75

Day 5: The Child 78

Day 6: The Yoke 80

Day 7: Ember Day #1 82

Day 8: The Lord's Prayer 85

Day 9: The Healer 88

Day 10: A Clean Slate 90

Day 11: The Woman at the Well 92

Day 12: Ten Lepers 94

Day 13: The A.C.T.S. Prayer 97

Day 14: Ember Day #2	99
Day 15: A Small Voice	101
Day 16: The Party	103
Day 17: Who Do You Say I Am?	106
Day 18: The Decision-Maker	108
Day 19: Loving Enemies	110
Day 20: The Worry List	112
Day 21: Ember Day #3	114
Day 22: Bread of Life	116
Day 23: A Contemplative Psalm	119
Day 24: The Traveler	121
Day 25: The A.C.T.S. Prayer Revisited	124
Day 26: The Beatitudes	126
Day 27: The Hitchhiker	128
Day 28: Ember Day #4	130
Day 29: The Lost Son Revisited	132
Day 30: The First Day (Of the Rest of Your Life)	135
About the Authors	139

ACKNOWLEDGMENTS

As you might expect, books on the practice of prayer require an ample supply of human guinea pigs—good-natured and patient souls who willingly subject themselves to the hits and misses of a work in progress.

Open Road began as a workshop we created in 2007 for the church we pastored in Penfield, New York. Over the years, church members and ministry leaders suffered through various iterations of the book, offering no small amount of encouragement and insights along the way. For their support and feedback, New Covenant has our unwavering gratitude.

A special note of thanks is also owed to the monks at the Abbey of the Genesee in Piffard, New York. The Trappists' knack for hospitality and regular conversations with the monastery's prior provided access to the contemplative way at a time when prayer seemed like more trouble than it was worth.

We're glad we were wrong. As it turns out, prayer is worth the trouble ... and then some.

1

INTRODUCTION

"… the kingdom of God is within you."

\- Luke 17:21

How would you describe prayer? Maybe some of these scenarios sound familiar:

- You want to pray more, but you struggle to integrate prayer into your daily routine. When you finally sit down for face time with the Almighty, you don't have a clue about how to make prayer interesting or meaningful.

- You pray semi-regularly, but nothing seems to happen. Rather than being a spiritually moving or mystical experience, prayer feels like one of the most boring things you've ever done.

- You've given up on the idea of praying consistently. Maybe someday—when the kids are older, when things aren't so busy at work, when pink frogs fall from the sky—you'll make prayer a priority. Until then, you'll just limp along, firing off the occasional prayer request when you really need something.

According to a recent Pew Research Center survey, nearly four out of five Americans say they pray occasionally (at least once a month). But relatively few of us experience the kind of prayer that produces joy, peace and connectedness with God.

Here's the elephant in the room, the uncomfortable reality that we try to ignore when it comes to prayer:

Most of us struggle to maintain a vibrant, active and spiritually enriching prayer life.

The good news is that prayer doesn't have to be difficult or boring.

In fact, prayer can be the most natural, fascinating and life-changing thing you have ever experienced.

Throughout history, ordinary people have searched for ways to connect with God through prayer. Coming from almost every background you can imagine, these spiritual explorers have described prayer in a variety of ways.

INTRODUCTION

A Journey Through a Castle

In the sixteenth century, Teresa of Avila, a holy woman and church reformer, envisioned prayer as a movement through a set of rooms in a castle.

As we travel across the courtyard, through the gates and into the rooms of the castle, we move closer to God and develop spiritual virtues like humility and perseverance.

In Teresa's work, *The Interior Castle*, the deepest levels of prayer are characterized by stillness, quiet and peace in the presence of God.

A Voyage Into the Unknown

John of the Cross, one of Teresa's followers, experienced prayer as an interaction with a God who is both close to us and far beyond our ability to comprehend.

For John, prayer and the indescribable mystery of God lead to a place of darkness (a "dark night of the soul") where we let go of the attachments and distractions that separate us from God.

"If a man wishes to be sure of the road he travels on," John said, "he must close his eyes and walk in the dark."

A World of Fire and Light

A fourteenth-century English churchman, Richard Rolle, believed that everyone is capable of having a dynamic, daily prayer life—not just pastors and priests, monks and nuns.

He saw prayer as a spiritual encounter in which the fire of God warms and illuminates the innermost parts of the soul. In Rolle's experience, a penetrating heat and sweetness accompanies the love of God in prayer.

Even though Teresa, John of the Cross and Rolle experienced prayer in different ways, everyone who has dared traverse the unfamiliar, uncharted territory of prayer agrees on one thing:

Prayer is like a road trip—a journey *into* God.

A "journey into God" sounds strange, maybe even a little scary. Does our road trip or journey into God mean that we're absorbed into God, like an ice cube melting in a bowl of chicken noodle soup?

Not at all. Instead, the journey into God is a journey home:

> Home is the place we feel safe and secure.
> Home is the place we feel loved and accepted.
> Home is the place where our lives make sense.

God is your soul's true home.

The journey home is a process of learning how to experience God so you are more mindful of his presence in your life.

INTRODUCTION

The Psalmist wrote:

> *Where can I go from your Spirit?*
> *Where can I flee from your presence?*
> *If I go up to the heavens, you are there;*
> *If I make my bed in the depths, you are there.*
> *If I rise on the wings of the dawn,*
> *If I settle on the far side of the sea,*
> *Even there your hand will guide me,*
> *Your right hand will hold me fast.*
> *If I say, "Surely the darkness will hide me*
> *And the light become night around me,"*
> *Even the darkness will not be dark to you;*
> *The night will shine like the day, for darkness is as*
> *Light to you.*
>
> - Psalm 139:7-12 (NIV)

God's presence surrounds you whether you know it or not. But your awareness of his presence? That's a different story.

Prayer nurtures an awareness of God's presence in the world around you and reshapes your busy life into a more spiritually grounded way of being.

Maybe you're starting from scratch, with a non-existent prayer life and little or no connection to God. Or maybe you just want to make your prayer life richer and more meaningful.

Either way, the next thirty days offer an opportunity to begin a journey into God—a journey that can change the way you experience life.

As you make progress on the road home to God, you will feel challenged and frustrated and confused and exhilarated—all at the same time. But you'll also start to have the kind of relationship with God you've always hoped was possible.

2

HOW TO USE THIS BOOK

The next thirty days could be the most important thirty days of your life.

That's probably hard to believe. After all, you're busy and a month will fly by in the blink of an eye. It's okay to be skeptical, but you need to know that *Open Road* was created with people like you in mind.

Plenty of books talk about prayer as a concept. The last thing you need is another resource that drones on about the theology of prayer, but never gets around to actually helping you develop a more consistent prayer life.

Yet that's exactly what *Open Road* is designed to do—to provide an "open road" to God by equipping you with the practical tools and exercises you need to integrate soulful prayer into your daily routine.

By setting aside just 15-20 minutes a day for prayer, you can develop a rich and stimulating spirituality that you can maintain for the rest of your life.

To help you get there, we've divided this book into two parts:

Part I teaches you how to make stimulating daily prayer a lived reality. Filled with practical tips and prayer techniques, these four chapters (one per week) walk you through the various elements of a well-balanced prayer life and start you on the road to a closer relationship with God.

Part II serves up creative, daily prayer exercises for your entire 30-day journey. Crafted for busy people, these exercises help you put the things you're learning into practice and allow you to enjoy regular, direct encounters with God.

There are many different ways to use the materials in this book. But you should know that the daily prayer exercises in Part II complement the weekly topics discussed in Part I.

We suggest reading the relevant chapter in Part I and then praying the corresponding exercises (found in Part II) for the next seven days. So ideally, your 30-day prayer journey might look something like this:

WEEK 1

Read: Chapter 4 – A Road Map: Making Room for God

Pray: Daily Exercises 1-7

WEEK 2

Read: Chapter 5 – On the Road: Starting Conversations

Pray: Daily Exercises 8-14

WEEK 3

Read: Chapter 6 – Gaining Speed: Using Intuition

Pray: Daily Exercises 15-21

WEEK 4

Read: Chapter 7 – Home: Finding Joy in God's Presence

Pray: Daily Exercises 22-30

+++

Again, the above schedule is just one way to use the materials. If you want to spend more time on a specific chapter or repeat a previous prayer exercise, feel free to add extra days to your journey.

The point isn't to follow a rigid 30-day schedule—it's to develop a habit of creative prayer that helps you recognize the presence of God in your life.

3

GROUND RULES FOR PRAYER

For people who aren't in the habit of keeping daily prayer times or doing creative prayer exercises, it's only natural to feel a little intimidated at the start of a 30-day prayer journey.

But if you set aside your preconceptions about what you think prayer *should* be, you will quickly discover the rich and vital experience that prayer *can* be.

Still not convinced? Here are a few ground rules to consider.

No Experience Necessary

Anyone can pray. If you already have a relationship with God and want to take it to the next level, the kind of prayer you will experience over the next thirty days is perfect for you.

But if you're starting from zero, new to Christian spirituality or want to learn more about how to live a dynamic, joy-filled life, you're also on the right track.

Even seekers who are exploring faith and spirituality for the first time will benefit from the next thirty days because there's no better way to know God than to interact with him through prayer.

The bottom line is that regardless of how much (or how little) you have prayed in the past, you will be surprised by the spiritual growth that happens when you integrate short, yet spiritually significant prayer times into your everyday routine.

But here's the catch: Prayer is kind of like playing a musical instrument. The more a violinist practices, the more adept she becomes at sharing melodies with the world.

Likewise, the more you pray, the more skilled you will become at sensing God's presence and sharing it with the rest of the world.

Prayer Is About Trying New Things

Some of the terms and techniques we discuss may be unfamiliar to you. But don't let unfamiliarity intimidate you or discourage you from trying new things.

The various methods of prayer we will cover have a solid biblical basis and have been practiced by other Christians going back to the time of the apostles. Even Jesus practiced many of the prayer techniques we talk about in this book, so don't be concerned that you are somehow offending God by the way you're praying.

For now, just know that this is not a typical course on prayer. You will encounter methods of praying that you haven't considered before, many of which rely heavily on your God-given gifts of imagination and intuition.

Give yourself over to the process and be open to encountering God in new and exciting ways.

There Are No Wrong Ways To Pray

If you're looking for a formula to draw you closer to God, you're going to be disappointed.

Everyone's prayer journey is different. Over the next month, you'll receive guidance and tips about how to pray. But ultimately, you will have to decide what works for you and what doesn't.

The upside is that you can't mess this up. Some days, prayer will be easy; other days, it will feel like a slog through wet cement. It's completely normal to feel frustrated or disappointed sometimes. Even people who have been praying for decades have bad prayer days.

Also, don't feel pressured to pray a certain way just because it worked for someone else. Experiment with various prayer techniques, evaluate how well they work and stick with the ones that increase your awareness of God's presence in the world.

Prayer Is A Never-Ending Journey

The next thirty days have the potential to change your life for the better by opening a door to a more spiritually authentic way of life.

However, that can only happen if you choose to treat this time not as a one-time event, but as the beginning of a lifelong journey that incorporates moments of creative prayer into your daily schedule.

Experts say it takes about a month to establish a new habit and that's what we're trying to create—a new habit of prayer that takes you deeper into God and leads you back to your soul's true home.

PART I

4

A ROAD MAP
MAKING ROOM FOR GOD

"... When you pray, go into your room, close the door and pray to your Father, who is unseen."

- Matthew 6:6

What's in your garage? Close your eyes and picture the items that are stored in your garage right now. (If you don't have a garage, try to picture the items stored in your attic, basement or closet.)

What do you see? Boxes? Paint cans? Maybe a lawnmower? In addition to bikes, tools and garden supplies, our garage contains boxes and containers filled with stuff we haven't used for years.

Statistically, there's a good chance that your garage is so full of clutter that you have to park at least one car in the driveway. Americans are packrats and the vast majority of us (experts say it's almost 80 percent) don't get rid of things we no longer use, cramming our garages, attics and basements with stuff we simply don't need anymore.

Unfortunately, our everyday lives look a lot like our garages. Job demands, family responsibilities and hobbies have our calendars bursting at the seams. It's hard to imagine trying to cram one more thing into our daily schedules.

How did we get ourselves into this mess? Part of the problem is that we're conditioned to avoid choices. We live under the illusion that we can have it all, so we run ourselves ragged trying to keep up with the crazy pace we've set for our lives.

But think about how ridiculous it is to store boxes of worthless junk safely *inside* your garage, while vehicles worth thousands of dollars are exposed to the elements *outside*.

Even though garages are built for cars, we've found a way to store everything except our cars inside of them.

In the same way that garages were created for cars, your life was created for God.

But somehow, you've filled your life with so many other things that now it's hard for God to find space. It's like he's standing outside your daily schedule, peeking through the windows and hoping that you'll find a way to let him in.

Although your life is hectic, it's possible (and necessary) to throw open the garage door of your soul and invite God to come inside.

But to do it, you'll need to rediscover a spiritual discipline that's as old as Christianity itself: solitude.

Solitude is the starting point for your journey into God.

There's a misperception that solitude and loneliness mean the same thing. The terms sound similar, but spiritual solitude and loneliness are actually as different as night and day.

> *Loneliness* is a place where we feel cut off from God and others, a hopeless place where we feel abandoned by everyone, even the people who are supposed to love us the most.
>
> *Solitude* is a place we deliberately go to connect with God. Instead of making us feel hopeless and abandoned, solitude draws us into a deeper relationship with God and creates much-needed space for him in our daily lives.

The Desert Fathers & Mothers

The desert fathers and mothers were men and women who experimented with radical solitude in the third and fourth centuries, during the years after the mainstreaming of Christianity by Constantine.

Even though the desert fathers and mothers pursued solitary lives in caves and other remote locations (some even lived on platforms mounted on the top of poles!), they rejected the notion that people had to live the way they did to experience solitude.

One of the desert mothers, Amma Syncletica, said:

> *There are many who live in the mountains and behave as if they were in the town, and they are wasting their time. It is possible to be a solitary in one's mind while living in a crowd, and it is possible for one who is a solitary to live in the crowd of his own thoughts.*

Does that sound impossible? Don't worry. Over the next few days, you're going to create a workable plan for experiencing daily solitude in your own life.

+++

EXERCISE: BUILDING RELATIONSHIPS

Think about someone you love. It could be your spouse, your child, your best friend, etc.:

- *How would you describe your relationship with this person? Is it close?*

- *What are some of the things that have made this relationship an important part of your life?*

- *If your relationship with this person was in trouble, what would you be willing to give up to make more time for him/her in your busy life?*

Healthy relationships are built on shared time, shared space and shared experiences—the same building blocks that create the foundation for a relationship with God.

Solitude helps you grow closer to God by making room for these building blocks in your unbelievably busy life.

Shared Time

Time spent in solitude is time that is devoted to developing and growing your relationship with God.

Community, or being around other people, is an important spiritual discipline. Without community, we risk narcissism, extremism and other *-isms* that tend to happen when we isolate ourselves from others.

But despite the need for community, there are some spiritual disciplines that have to be practiced alone, including daily prayer and reflection.

The way you choose to incorporate solitude into your schedule is entirely up to you. You might find it helpful to experience solitude at the same time each day, e.g., before work, during lunch hour or after dinner.

Then again, you may find it easier to vary the times you experience solitude and sneak off to be alone whenever you feel the need to connect with God.

The amount of time you spend in solitude isn't important. Even a few minutes a day can make a big difference in your awareness of God's presence in your life.

+++

EXERCISE: FINDING TIME FOR SOLITUDE

For busy people, solitude seems like an impossible task. But by asking the right questions about your daily routines, you can identify the best times for solitude:

- *God deserves your best, not your leftovers. What time of day are you at your best? Before the kids wake up? During your morning coffee break? After dinner?*

- *Multi-tasking and solitude don't mix. On a normal day, when are you least likely to be disturbed or distracted?*

- *Pick a 20-minute time to experience solitude each day. This is only a starting point—it can change if you discover that the time you select doesn't work.*

+++

If you're looking for an ideal time slot for solitude, stop now. It doesn't exist. You may need to shift your priorities to find 15-20 minutes in your schedule for solitude and prayer.

Also, keep in mind that the goal for solitude isn't "down time" or a personal time-out. It's to give God a foothold in your schedule by setting aside a small block of time every day for prayer, reflection and meditation.

Shared Space

Making physical space for prayer is just as important as making time for prayer.

Long distance relationships rarely last because relationships require shared space to grow. Solitude is sacred space, holy ground, a meeting place where you go to meet with God.

But wait a minute. If God's presence is all around me, I shouldn't have to go anywhere to meet him, right?

It's not that simple. It's true that you can experience solitude anywhere—in your kitchen, at your cubicle, even in your car. But to experience the kind of solitude that builds relationships, many people find it helpful to designate a space that is separated from the distractions that are going on around them.

Think about it: When you go on a date, which venue is better for getting to know someone—a rock concert or an intimate candlelight dinner?

Although a rock concert might be fun, a candlelight dinner is a better atmosphere for building a close relationship with another person.

Depending on your circumstances, you may have to get creative about consecrating a space for solitude.

The possibilities for solitude include:

- Your favorite recliner
- A designated "quiet room" where Mommy goes to talk to God
- A corner of the basement that serves as your "fortress of solitude"
- A local park or nature space
- Your desk or cubicle, with a special image displayed on your computer screen

The place you choose to pray isn't important. Nothing about the space itself makes it sacred or holy. It's sacred because it's the place you've set aside (or consecrated) to function as a meeting place with God.

+++

EXERCISE: FINDING SACRED SPACE

Your sacred space can be a familiar place or it can be an entirely new place you discover for prayer.

Here are a few questions to help you identify the right place for daily prayer:

- *Where do you feel safest and most free to be yourself? In your home? In nature? In a religious space?*

- *Can you think of a safe, distraction-free location where you can go to spend time with God? If not, can you think of something you can do to consecrate a public space for solitude?*

Shared Experiences

Shared experiences are also important for building healthy relationships. Why? Because experiences are touch points that create common history with the people that matter to us.

Think about the relationship you share with your spouse or a close friend. You probably don't remember specific events in the relationship as a day on the calendar, but rather as "the day we moved into the house on Chestnut Street" or "the time the car broke down in a snowstorm."

Your relationship with God works the same way. The shared experiences that happen in solitude establish the foundation of your history with God, and out of that history, relationship-builders like trust and understanding begin to emerge.

The best way to remember your shared experiences is to write them down in a prayer journal.

If you're not in the habit of journaling, recording your experiences with God may feel strange. But you're not writing the next great American novel. In fact, you're the only person who will ever read your journal entries.

The purpose of your journal is to simply record the things that happen during daily prayer times. It only takes a few words or sentences to help you recall the high points (and low points) of your shared experiences with God.

Prayer Pointers: Week 1

Quality vs. Quantity

As you begin your journey into God, it's tempting to believe that you have to pray for long periods of time to make progress.

In fact, long periods of prayer are difficult (even for people with lots of prayer experience) and you will probably become distracted or discouraged if you try to do too much.

A better approach is to start by setting aside just 15-20 minutes for prayer each day.

Prayer "Warm-Ups"

You're not a machine. You can't flip a switch and instantly transition from the crazy pace of your busy life to a peaceful, meditative state.

To get in the right mental space for prayer, you may need to do a "warm-up" exercise to quiet your thoughts. Although these tried-and-true exercises are ideal for preparing to pray, they are also tools you can use to periodically decompress and refocus throughout the day.

> Breathing. A few deep breaths can make a big difference in your ability to relax and focus. Breathe deeply through your nose, hold it for a few seconds and then release it through your mouth. As you inhale, imagine that you are drawing God's

strength and peace into your tired body and mind. As you exhale, imagine that you are letting go of your worries, your concerns and (most of all) your to-do list.

Empty Cup/Full Cup. Sit comfortably in a chair with your hands resting lightly on your knees. Imagine you are holding a cup in your hands, a cup that contains all of the things that stress you out. With your eyes closed, turn your hands palms-down and imagine all of your concerns spilling out of the cup and out of your mind. Next, turn your hands palms-up and imagine your "cup" being filled with good things from God. When a concern creeps back into your mind, repeat the process.

Muscle Relaxation. Starting from a comfortable position, tense the muscles in your feet, count to five and release the tension. As your muscles relax, feel concerns and worries leave your body and your mind. Next, move up to the lower legs and repeat the process. Keep working your way up the body until you have reached the top of your head and you feel completely relaxed.

Keep Moving

Sometimes God seems far away and it feels like your attempts to find him in prayer are pointless. You'll probably feel discouraged at least once this week as you try to integrate solitude into your life.

But it will get easier! If you miss a day, don't beat yourself up over it. Just make a commitment to let nothing stand in the way of solitude and spending time with God tomorrow.

5

ON THE ROAD
STARTING CONVERSATIONS

*"Morning, noon, and night I cry out ...
and the Lord hears my voice."*

- Psalm 55:17

Prayer is the art of making conversation with God. Sound easy? It isn't. Because chatting with the creator of the universe is trickier than making small talk at a cocktail party.

Does God even care what you have to say? And if he does care, then why have your past attempts at starting conversations with God been such disasters?

Meaningless repetition, endless silences and one-sided dialogues have left too many of us with the impression that a conversation with God is a huge waste of time.

But before you give up on prayer, consider this: If you can have interesting conversations with your friends, your spouse or your hair stylist, you can have interesting conversations with God.

- At the end of a long day, how do you start a conversation with your spouse or significant other?
- What do you talk about when you get together with friends and family members?
- What topics came up in conversation the last time you visited the hair salon or barbershop?

The kinds of conversations you have with your spouse, your friends and your hair stylist are the kinds of conversations God wants to have with you every day.

- When *spouses* talk, they share the high points and low points of their day, and sometimes discuss intimate details about their lives.
- When *friends* get together they catch up on what's happened since they last saw each other.
- And the *hair salon*? In most salons and barbershops, few topics of conversation are off-limits.

Prayer is the vehicle for sharing your life with God—the good, the bad and the ugly. Since each day brings a new set of possibilities and challenges into your life, you should always have something new to talk about with God.

EXERCISE: DEAR DIARY

Find a blank page in your journal. If you don't have a journal, a blank sheet of paper will work fine.

At the top of the page, write the words, "Dear Diary." Then write down a brief description of your day and any unusual events that occurred.

Now read your diary entry (either out loud or silently), substituting the words "Dear God" for "Dear Diary."

Believe it or not, you've just started a great conversation with God by sharing the kinds of details that create close relationships.

+++

Relationships bring context to conversations. When we're in an extended, healthy relationship, we feel safe to discuss extremely personal topics.

As your relationship with God grows, your conversations will become deeper and more meaningful. Although you'll still talk about ordinary, everyday things, you will also find yourself discussing increasingly personal thoughts and life experiences.

But there's a the catch. Every married couple knows that long-term relationships present special challenges for communication. Although it's a struggle to keep the conversation fresh, people who have been married for decades still find a way to share interesting conversations.

So how do old married couples do it? They make an intentional effort to talk about the details of their lives and learn new things about each other.

Infinite Variety

In the 1993 comedy, *Groundhog Day*, Bill Murray's character lives February 2nd over and over again. Day after day, he has the same conversations with the same people in the small town of Punxsutawney, Pennsylvania.

Before long, the monotony overwhelms him. He stops talking to people entirely and eventually has a bit of a psychotic episode.

Sound familiar? It should. Sometimes prayer mirrors Murray's dilemma in *Groundhog Day*. After having the same conversation with God day after day, we become so exasperated that we just stop trying.

A robust prayer life is hard work. Monotonous and repetitive prayer can often be traced to "prayer ruts"—shortcuts that let us be lazy and avoid the effort that makes prayer interesting.

Prayer Rut #1: The Wish List

> When we were kids, many of us learned how to pray by reciting a nightly "wish list" of needs and wants to God. There's nothing wrong with wish lists. In fact, God encourages us to tell him about the things we need and want in prayer.

The problem is that some people's prayer lives never move beyond the wish list. For some folks, prayer is just an opportunity to ask God for things they can't achieve on their own. When God doesn't answer their prayers in the timeframe or manner they desire, they get bored and give up.

Unanswered wish list prayers can also lead to wacky theology. If your relationship with God is limited to what he does or doesn't do for you, sooner or later you'll start to question his commitment to the relationship—especially when the requests on your wish list aren't granted.

It's important to maintain balance in your conversations with God. *Supplication* (the wish list) is a valid and important part of the conversation. But so are *Confession* (telling God about your failures and shortcomings), *Worship* (appreciating God for who he is), *Thankfulness* (expressing gratitude for the things God has done for you) and *Intercession* (praying for other people's needs and the needs of the world).

Prayer Rut #2: The Formula

At the other end of the spectrum, there are people who are so obsessed with avoiding a one-dimensional prayer life that their conversations with God have turned rigid.

Regardless of how the conversation with God unfolds, they adhere to a strict personal prayer "formula" and feel guilty if the conversation goes off course.

A formulaic prayer life can also be boring. It's no wonder that this way of praying doesn't lead to a vibrant relationship with God because it's lifeless, stale and forced.

Although it's important to maintain balance in your conversations with God, it's more important to give the Spirit the freedom to take the conversation in whatever direction he desires.

There are no firm rules governing how you should pray at any given time. One day your prayer might cover the entire range of prayer topics: *Supplication*, *Confession*, *Worship*, *Thankfulness* and *Intercession*. The next day you might spend the entire time on just one topic. What you pray about is entirely up to you and God.

But pay attention to how the conversation unfolds and try to maintain a balance in your prayer life rather than trying to do it all every time you pray.

Holy Curiosity

Human beings are curious creatures. Over the centuries, our curiosity has led to major discoveries in medicine, physics, astronomy and other fields.

Several months before his death, Albert Einstein told *Life* magazine editor, William Miller:

> *One cannot help but be in awe when he contemplates the mysteries of eternity, of life, of the marvelous structure of reality. It is enough if one tries merely to comprehend a little of this mystery everyday. Never lose a <u>holy curiosity</u>.*

Einstein might have been on to something. Curiosity is a sacred treasure God has dropped in your lap to help you discover new things. If curiosity can motivate scientists to explore the universe, just imagine how useful it can be for exploring the mystery of God.

We have to get it out of our heads that prayer has to be rigid to be real. Your curiosity is a holy thing, a gift from God that helps you find your way back to him.

If you want to enjoy a more interesting prayer life, you have to let your curiosity shape your conversations with God. When you give curiosity free rein in prayer, you learn new things about God and yourself.

For example, instead of just telling God that a coworker annoys you, your curiosity might cause you to ask God why the coworker is so annoying. Although God may show you things you haven't noticed about your coworker, it's just as likely (or even more likely) that he'll show you things you haven't noticed about yourself and the way you relate to your coworker.

And instead of just praying for the poor, your curiosity might lead to an in-depth conversation with God about the root causes of poverty and God's heart for the poor. Prayer might even become the place where

God speaks to you about becoming more actively involved in groups or ministries that serve the poor.

You get the picture. God wants to hear everything that is on your mind. Prayer is about your relationship with God, and for that relationship to stay healthy, you need to bring your curiosity to the conversation.

The key to igniting your curiosity is to recognize that through prayer, heaven is now. God is your soul's true home, but he's not just a home that you return to after you die. He's a home that you can experience right here, right now.

+++

EXERCISE: "WHEN I GET TO HEAVEN"

Make a list of three things you want to ask God about when you get to heaven.

Why wait? Ask God about these three things the next time you pray and listen for his response.

+++

Brutal Honesty

God always has the upper hand in prayer. He knows what you're thinking and feeling even before you know it yourself. The idea of brutal honesty in prayer might sound silly because God knows the truth even if you aren't willing to talk about it.

But it's a little more complicated than that. Even though God knows your thoughts and feelings, his awareness of them doesn't change your need to talk about them. If you're going to make progress on your journey into God, you need to be completely transparent in prayer.

What kind of a marriage would you have if you held back your deepest, truest feelings from your spouse? Not a very good one. It would be a superficial marriage based on omissions and partial truths. Your relationship with God works the same way.

What does brutal honesty with God really look like? Here's how Francois Fenelon, a seventeenth-century French monk, described it in a letter to a friend:

> **Talk with God about the thoughts of which your heart is full.** *If you enjoy the presence of God, if you feel drawn to love Him, tell Him so. Such sensible passion will make the time of prayer fly without exhausting you, for all you'll have to do is say what you feel.*
>
> **But what are you to do in the times of dryness, inner resistance, and coldness?** *Do the same thing. Say equally what is in your heart! Tell God ... that things concerning Him exhaust you ... that you long to leave Him for whatever comes your way, and that you won't feel happy until you've left Him and can turn your time into thinking about yourself. Tell Him all the evil you know about yourself.*

When you tell Him about your miseries, ask Him to cure them. Say to Him, 'My God, you see my ingratitude, my inconsistency. Take my heart for I don't know how to give it to You. Give me an inner distaste for external things; give me crosses necessary to bring me back under your leadership. Have mercy on me in spite of myself!'

In either of these two states I've described, tell Him without hesitation everything that comes into your head, with simplicity and familiarity, as a little child sitting on its mother's knee.

Honesty in prayer is as simple as telling God whatever you are thinking or feeling, even if it makes you feel ashamed and vulnerable.

Unlike other relationships you may have experienced, God won't exploit your vulnerability or use your shame as an excuse to punish you. Over and over again, he will use your honesty to make your relationship with him even stronger.

Prayer Pointers: Week 2

Creativity

Curiosity is a prerequisite for prayer. As your prayers become more curious, your God-given creativity will begin to emerge and you will start thinking about all kinds of ways to draw closer to God in prayer.

Don't stifle your creativity! Imagination is a gift from God and random thoughts may be his way of helping you on your journey. Feel free to explore, experiment and hold on to the methods that are most effective.

Conversation Starters

Conversation starters help launch prayer times. Good conversation starters include Scripture (e.g., a favorite Psalm or gospel passage), a ready-made prayer (e.g., the Lord's Prayer) or a spiritual declaration (e.g., the Apostles' Creed).

This week's prayer exercises provide opportunities to experiment with a few conversation starters. Avoid rushing through these conversation starters and give God the freedom to guide the conversation. Linger over words or phrases that stand out and let them become starting points for conversations with God using your own words.

Mindfulness

The goal of your 30-day prayer journey is to help you feel God's presence in your life. Daily prayer is a type of spiritual conditioning. It helps you learn how to recognize God's voice and become spiritually attune to his presence.

But to really experience God's presence in your life, you need to get into the habit of pausing throughout the day to pay attention to what God is saying and doing.

It only takes a few seconds, but periodic "STOP, LOOK and LISTEN" moments can transform the seemingly ordinary events of your day from mundane to mystical.

What You Might Be Experiencing

Now that you have at least a week of regular, daily prayer under your belt, you might be experiencing a few prayer-related challenges:

Boredom (*Acedia*)

> It's not uncommon to experience a certain amount of boredom during prayer times. Even the desert fathers and mothers—history's version of professional prayer practitioners—occasionally experienced restlessness, or *acedia*, in their pursuit of God.
>
> The advice for people experiencing *acedia* has always been to stick with it! In other words, the best way to overcome boredom is to press through it until you reach the other side.

If boredom continues, you may need to evaluate the length of your prayer times. Long periods of prayer can be a recipe for boredom, especially if you are just starting to integrate prayer into your daily routine.

Euphoria

At the other end of the spectrum, you may be experiencing euphoria. Euphoria is a feeling of exhilaration, an excitement that comes from experiencing God's presence in a fresh way or maybe even for the very first time.

The problem with euphoria is that it doesn't last. Eventually, the excitement that you're feeling now will diminish as prayer becomes a normal part of your daily routine.

When the initial wave of euphoria disappears, some people feel a huge letdown, as if God has either abandoned them or lured them in under false pretenses.

Neither of those things is true. By now, you should be starting to realize that your relationship with God is unlike any other relationship in your life.

There will be highs and lows, and the sudden disappearance of euphoria is not an indication that God is unhappy with you. It's just a normal part of the journey home.

6

GAINING SPEED
USING INTUITION

"Deep calls to deep ..."

- Psalm 42:7

Healthy relationships are built on conversations and dialogue. But learning how to talk to God is just the first step. You also need to learn how to hear God when he talks to you.

The problem with hearing God is that it's virtually impossible to be absolutely, 100% sure that you're hearing God's side of the conversation accurately. As you continue to make prayer a part of your everyday routine, it's only a matter of time before you have serious doubts about whether the things you're hearing are actually from God.

Unfortunately, there's a lot of confusion out there about what it means to hear God. At one end of the spectrum, you'll find overly confident people who consistently use phrases like, "God told me," so they can manipulate others to their point of view. At the other end of the spectrum, you'll find people who have difficulty believing God speaks to them at all.

So what's the deal?

- Does God really speak to us?
- And if he does, is it possible to hear his voice and understand what he's trying to tell us?

The answer to both of these questions is a definite "yes." God does speak to us and we can hear his voice. But to understand what he's saying, we need to stop approaching the task of hearing God's voice like it's a science. It's not a science. It's a spiritual art.

Knowing for sure that you've heard God speak to you is impossible for a very simple reason:

Hearing God is always an act of faith.

It would be great if God picked up the phone or sent a text message every now and then, but that's not how he operates. Instead, God communicates with us in a "still small voice."

> *A great and strong wind tore into the mountains and broke the rocks in pieces before the Lord, but the Lord was not in the wind; and after the wind an earthquake, but the Lord was not in the earthquake; and after the earthquake a fire, but the Lord was not in the fire; and after the fire <u>a still small voice</u>.*
>
> - 1 Kings 19:11-12 (NKJV)

Hearing God is kind of like listening to whispers. God could get your attention with a burning bush if he wanted to, but he usually speaks through whispers in prayer.

As you become more adept at recognizing God's presence, it will become a little easier to recognize his "small voice." But even then, you'll have to exercise faith to believe God is really speaking to you through the words, thoughts and impressions you receive when you pray.

How God Speaks To Us

Although God has been known to speak through dramatic events, you probably won't experience anything like that the next time you pray. It's more likely that you will hear God's voice in more subtle ways.

Through Silence and Intuition

Silence sets the stage for hearing God's voice. The cacophony of sounds in your fast-paced daily life makes it difficult (if not impossible) to distinguish God's voice from the multitude of other voices vying for your attention. The silence experienced in solitude turns down the volume and tunes your soul into God's frequency.

As you spend time with God in silence, you'll eventually sense that God is drawing your attention toward a specific theme or issue. When that happens, your first reaction may be to write it off as a figment of your imagination.

But isn't your imagination a gift from God?

And when you use your imagination, aren't you simply expanding the boundaries of your awareness to consider ideas, perspectives and directions you hadn't considered before?

That's exactly what hearing God is all about—opening your mind and heart to allow God to speak to you in fresh and exciting ways.

Hearing God requires us to engage our intuitive selves rather than our analytical selves. Our culture, education and careers teach us to value hard analysis and facts more than feelings.

But intuition—the ability to feel or sense things you can never prove—is essential for hearing God.

Intuition is the ability to comprehend thoughts and ideas that aren't staring you directly in the face. Even people who rely on empirical data have learned the value of trusting intuition. In fact, many scientists admit that intuition is central to their work.

In *Anatomy of Reality*, here's how Jonas Salk, the researcher who discovered and developed the polio vaccine, described the role of intuition:

> *It is always with excitement that I wake up in the morning wondering what my intuition will toss up to me, like gifts from the sea. I work with it and rely on it. It's my partner.*

Like imagination, intuition is a God-given gift, a valuable partner to guide you in prayer. Rather than quickly dismissing thoughts and impressions, open your mind to the possibility that God may be asking you to use intuition to hear his voice.

+++

EXERCISE: HUNCHES & FEELINGS

When was the last time you had a hunch or a feeling that God might be up to something in your life?

How did you react to your hunch? Did you dismiss it? Or did you consider the idea that God might be trying to speak to you?

+++

Through Scripture

Another way God speaks to us is through Scripture. Many of us have been taught to use Scripture as a resource for study, theology or maybe even sermon preparation.

But Scripture also has another purpose. With the right approach, it can serve as a tool for listening to God. Frequently, the Bible can help you hear something that is highly relevant to your personal circumstances.

Although you probably didn't realize it, the daily prayer exercises in Part II have been training you to hear God through a spiritual practice called *Lectio Divina* (or "divine reading").

Lectio Divina (pronounced "lek-see-oh di-veen-a") first appeared in Christianity around 200 A.D. The early Christians developed *Lectio Divina* as a way to engage God in a conversation and hear his voice more clearly. Today, Christians around the world practice *Lectio Divina* for the same reasons.

In its purest form, *Lectio Divina* has four stages: *Lectio, Meditatio, Oratio* and *Contemplatio*:

1. *Lectio* (Reading) – In the first stage of *Lectio Divina*, you select a short passage of Scripture and read it several times. The passage should be short and potentially useful (e.g., "begat" passages usually aren't good grist for the prayer mill). It also helps to read the passage out loud at least once.

2. *Meditatio* (Meditation) – After you've read the passage several times, meditate on its meaning and how it applies to your life. Don't try to study the passage! Instead, look for words, phrases or images that jump out at you.

3. *Oratio* (Response) – *Oratio* is your response to God. Although your response can take a variety of forms, use your intuition to "feel" your way through it. A carefully formulated prayer usually isn't as helpful as starting a candid and informal conversation with God about the passage or the words and images he brought to mind during the *Meditatio* stage.

4. *Contemplatio* (Contemplation) – In the final stage, completely open your heart and mind to God. Although God has been speaking to you throughout the entire process, his voice becomes clearer during this stage as you totally surrender to his presence.

Through Words and Images

God frequently speaks to us through words and mental images. When God speaks to us with words, we usually don't hear the words audibly. But we can sense them in our minds.

It's possible that the words we hear are constructs of our own making. Basically, we could just be telling ourselves what we want to hear. But it's also possible (even likely) that the words we hear are God's way of communicating with us.

Do the words and phrases you hear during prayer originate in your imagination? Maybe. But that doesn't mean they aren't from God because God uses our imagination to speak to us, drawing our attention beyond the realm of material and finite things to the realm of spiritual and transcendent ones.

Likewise, it's not unusual to encounter mental images during prayer. These images include things like people, places, objects, etc.

For example, you might experience a mental image of Jesus talking with you. Or you might find yourself remembering an image of a place or person that is important to you.

Since you haven't deliberately called these images to mind, you have to allow for the possibility that God is trying to tell you something through them.

+++

EXERCISE: SEEING & HEARING GOD

What do you see and hear when you pray? Do you experience any recurring words or images in prayer?

What do those words or images represent? Is it possible that God is trying to get your attention about something?

+++

Separating Diamonds From Daydreams

Some of the things you hear during prayer actually won't originate with God. Although you should never immediately dismiss anything, there are ways to distinguish divine "diamonds" from ordinary daydreams.

Generally, if what you're hearing is actually from God, it will have the following characteristics:

Depth

Depth is one of the first criteria to apply when you're trying to decide whether something you've heard is from God.

The Psalmist describes God's conversations with us as *"deep calling to deep."* If a thought, concept or understanding is too "deep" or insightful to come from you, it should pique your interest and make you wonder whether God is trying to speak from the "depth" of his being to the "depth" of yours.

Along the same lines, try to pay attention to things that seem to come from left field during prayer. If a word, thought or image suddenly pops into your head for no good reason, consider the possibility that it might be from God.

Consistency

When you believe God is saying something to you in prayer, make a point of writing it down and returning to it during later prayer times.

God doesn't change his mind, so if it's really from him, he will reinforce the thought no matter how many times you talk with him about it.

Far too many people make big decisions or take drastic actions based on something they believe God has spoken to them just once. No one hears God perfectly, so it's important to look for consistency as you move forward in prayer.

For really big decisions, it may be appropriate to revisit the topic over a period of weeks or months—to set aside a season of time to discern what God is saying to you.

Confirmation

Confirmation is a safety net. When you believe you've heard from God, it's always a good idea to look for confirmation before you do anything.

Everything that God speaks to you will be consistent with Scripture. For example, if you think God is telling you to rob a bank or sleep with your best friend's spouse, you can be sure that you haven't heard from God.

God also uses other people (e.g., friends, family members and spiritual advisors) to confirm the messages he communicates through prayer.

If you think God is saying something important to you, run it by people you trust and ask them to pray about it, too. In addition to confirming (or not confirming) what you think God is saying to you, they may offer additional insights about your situation or decision.

PRAYER POINTERS: WEEK 3

Trust Your Intuition

Life conditions you to disregard your intuition and only pay attention to things you can see, hear or touch.

But to hear God's voice, you need to engage your intuition and exercise it on a daily basis.

Don't immediately dismiss the thoughts and impressions you receive in prayer. Ruminate and pray over them until it becomes obvious whether or not God is really behind them.

Be Patient

The inability to hear God speak can be frustrating. But sooner or later, everyone experiences dry periods and times when God suddenly seems to go silent.

If you are finding it difficult to hear God speak to you, hang in there. It doesn't mean he has abandoned you or loves you any less.

Use Your Journal

Your journal can be a great tool for amplifying the volume of God's voice and clarifying the meaning of the things he is saying to you.

When you put the thoughts and impressions you receive during prayer on paper, you can gain clarity about the messages God is trying to communicate to you.

Sometimes God even continues the conversation while you're writing about it.

7

HOME
FINDING JOY IN GOD'S PRESENCE

"Be still and know ..."

- Psalm 46:10

Over the past few weeks, your journey into God has passed through several aspects of prayer:

In Week One, you were challenged to make space in your life for prayer, to find a time and a place for solitude. Although you could use more peace and quiet in your life, the goal of solitude isn't "down time," but a vibrant, active relationship with God through prayer.

In Week Two, you learned how to initiate conversations with God. While many of us have been taught that prayer is either one-dimensional ("the wish list") or rigid ("the formula"), conversational prayer opens the door to a tapestry of spiritual disciplines including worship, thankfulness, confession, supplication and intercession.

In Week Three, you discovered how to hear God as he speaks to you through words, images and impressions. You learned that hearing God is always an act of faith. It requires you to exercise your God-given gift of intuition and examine what you believe God is saying to you through a process of discernment.

The lessons you have learned are mile markers on your journey into God—your journey home. Together, they have prepared you to experience a deeper awareness of God's presence in your life.

These lessons have also led you to yet another facet of a balanced life of prayer: being still with God.

Over the centuries, Christians have experienced this type of prayer in a number of ways. Today, it is most commonly referred to as the prayer of simplicity, the prayer of stillness or just "contemplative prayer."

Contemplative prayer is a wordless conversation, a deliberate plunge into the depths of God's silence. In the midst of this silence, we completely surrender ourselves to God. Our agenda is entirely abandoned as we give ourselves over to God, wholly and unconditionally.

How Contemplative Prayer Works

Until now, you've been taking baby steps toward praying in stillness.

In addition to learning how to create solitude and maintain a balanced prayer life, you have gradually improved your ability to quiet your thoughts through daily warm-up exercises—activities that also happen to represent the first step in contemplative prayer.

Step 1: Centering

The first step in contemplative prayer involves centering ourselves as we prepare for an encounter with God's presence. Often referred to as "recollection," the centering step restores our distracted and fragmented minds into a coherent whole, ready to receive what God has in store for us.

Centering yourself can be tricky. Begin by doing a warm-up exercise like "empty cup/full cup." From there, you may find it useful to ask God to give you a word to use as a focal point.

Some Christians use the word "Jesus" to focus their thoughts during this step. They slowly and quietly repeat "Jesus" in their minds until their worries, concerns and "to-do" lists have slipped from their consciousness. When a distraction appears, simply return to the word "Jesus" to re-center your thoughts on God's presence.

As you do this, your mind will gradually become calmer and less cluttered. You're not emptying your thoughts to turn your mind over to just any spiritual influence. You're turning your mind—in fact your entire being—over to God in an act of love, trust and devotion.

At some point, you will begin to clearly sense God's presence surrounding you. That's a good thing. It means that you have successfully quieted your thoughts and distractions, and you're ready to move on to the next step.

Step 2: Stillness

After you have centered yourself, you have done all you can do to set the stage for an encounter with God. Now, your prayer is in the Holy Spirit's hands. From this point forward, your sole task will be to remain still, silenced and attentive to the movements of the Spirit.

You are not sedate or disengaged, but acutely aware of God's loving warmth. For reasons you can't explain, you have a deep sense of God's love being poured out to you—and your love being poured back to him.

In this place, God is doing something that transcends words. He is working on your soul like a potter shaping a piece of clay. Although the clay doesn't understand what is happening to it, it is being transformed into something beautiful.

Likewise, although you can't articulate what is taking place, you know that something beautiful is happening between you and God.

The experience of God's presence during this stage of prayer can stay with you long after your prayer time has ended. Throughout the day, you may return to an abiding sense that God is with you and in you, helping you see the world—and your life—through his eyes.

Step 3: Spiritual Ecstasy

Occasionally, contemplative prayer leads to something called, "spiritual ecstasy." Ecstasy, like the previous step, is entirely in God's hands and for most of us, it's the exception rather than the rule. It's not unusual for individuals to never experience spiritual ecstasy, even after decades of prayerful living.

The best way to describe spiritual ecstasy is that it's a taste of heaven on earth. Those who have experienced it describe it as being transported to a different place, much like John's experience at the beginning of the book of Revelation.

In the seventeenth century, a Dutch Protestant named Theodore Brakel described his experience of spiritual ecstasy this way:

> *I was ... transported into such a state of joy and my thoughts were so drawn upward that, seeing God with the eyes of my soul, I felt one with him. I felt myself transported into God's being and at the same time I was so filled with joy, peace, and sweetness, that I cannot express it. With my spirit I was entirely in heaven for two or three days.*

It's hard to imagine anyone who is serious about God not wanting to have that kind of experience. But if it never happens for you, don't be discouraged. Your goal shouldn't be an otherworldly experience. It should be a close and constant relationship with God.

Contemplative Prayer: Things To Think About

Contemplative prayer is one of the most rewarding types of prayer you can experience. But it's also one of the least understood.

To fully appreciate the value of contemplative prayer as a regular spiritual discipline, there are some things you need to keep in mind.

Contemplative prayer is about union with God.

Some people find it difficult to accept the idea that a healthy prayer life results in union with God. The word "union" is frequently misinterpreted to mean absorption into a divine energy of the universe or something else that sounds incompatible with orthodox Christian beliefs.

But that's not the kind of union we're talking about. In contemplative prayer, both you and God retain your individual identities. You don't become God and God definitely doesn't become you. Instead, contemplative prayer is the practical manifestation of something Jesus calls us to experience the gospel of John:

> *"Abide in me as I abide in you."*
>
> - John 15:4

You can't produce God's presence.

One of the most frustrating aspects of contemplative prayer is that it's largely out of your control. But if you think about it, isn't that the point?

In contemplative prayer, we completely surrender ourselves to God. Our agendas, our thoughts and our priorities are set aside as we trust God with our entire being. Since we've freely given ourselves over to God, what happens during contemplative prayer is entirely in God's hands.

You can prepare for God's presence, but you can't produce it. Apart from trying to maintain a stilled and quiet mind, you can do nothing—the outcome is completely dependent on God.

From a practical standpoint, contemplative prayer sometimes results in a strong sense of God's presence and sometimes it doesn't. Again, you're not a machine, and occasionally (or not so occasionally) you may find it difficult to quiet your thoughts.

But even when you are able to quiet your thoughts, there will be times when it just doesn't happen. Don't get upset about it. Instead, accept it for what it is and pick up again on a different day.

Contemplative prayer leads to self-discovery.

Once you have made contemplative prayer a regular practice, don't be surprised if God uses it to address unresolved issues in your life.

Although you'll learn new things about yourself, this process of self-discovery can be humbling and even painful at times.

God sometimes uses contemplative prayer as a tool for surfacing issues you have worked hard to ignore. In many cases, this kind of prayer is the venue God uses to address problems that we have been avoiding and perform inner healing in our lives.

The time to reflect on what God is doing through contemplative prayer happens after your prayer time has ended. Journaling is a valuable tool, but be alert for unexpected insights as you go about the ordinary routines of your day.

PRAYER POINTERS: WEEK 4

Baby Steps

Contemplative prayer may feel a little awkward, especially if this kind of prayer is new to you. Like any new activity, it's best to begin with baby steps.

Dedicate a few minutes each day to contemplative prayer and gradually increase the length of your prayer as you become more comfortable with it.

Balance

Contemplative prayer should complement other forms of prayer—not replace them. Many people find it useful to end their normal prayer times with a period of contemplative prayer.

It's also possible to dedicate some prayer sessions to conversational prayer and others to contemplative prayer.

Regardless of when you decide to pray contemplatively, the important thing is to integrate it into a balanced and well-rounded prayer life.

Spiritual Direction

Contemplative prayer has the potential to open the door to issues you may not be prepared to deal with on your own. Over the years, prayer-minded people have found it helpful to seek out a spiritual director to clarify how God is moving in their prayer lives.

A spiritual director is not a counselor, but someone who helps deepen your relationship with God and find answers to questions of a spiritual nature.

As you continue to progress in prayer, you might find it useful to periodically meet with someone for direction, guidance and support.

PART II

Day 1

THE MUSTARD SEED

Warm-Up

Find a comfortable, quiet place where you won't be disturbed so you can be completely present to God. If it's difficult to quiet your thoughts, try one of the prayer warm-up exercises (e.g., breathing, empty cup/full cup, muscle relaxation) to help you get started.

Reading: Mark 4:30-34

Jesus said that something as small as a mustard seed is capable of amazing things. As you read the following parable, imagine that you are among the peasants and farmers hearing Jesus speak for the first time.

> *(Jesus said), 'With what can we compare the kingdom of God, or what parable will we use for it? It is like a mustard seed, which, when sown upon the ground, is the smallest of all the seeds on earth; yet when it is sown it grows up and becomes the greatest of all*

shrubs, and puts forth large branches, so that the birds of the air can make nests in its shade.' With many such parables he spoke the word to them, as they were able to hear it; he did not speak to them except in parables, but he explained everything in private to his disciples.

For Prayer & Reflection

1. Mustard seeds are less than a millimeter in diameter. But despite their small size, mustard seeds add zing to the food we eat. How do you relate to God? Is your relationship dull and boring, or is it spicy and full of life?

2. **Read the parable again.** In the gospel of Luke, Jesus tells us that the kingdom of God isn't out there somewhere. According to Jesus, *"the kingdom of God is in you."* Do you believe him? What do you think it will take for the mustard seed of faith inside you to grow into a meaningful experience with God? Can you imagine how God might use your relationship with him to help others, (or as Jesus says, to make "nests" for the birds of the air in your branches)?

3. Remain silent for a few more minutes. Ask God to speak with you about whatever is on his mind. If you have any worries or concerns, tell them to God and listen for a response.

4. When you're done, don't forget to record your thoughts, impressions and experiences in your journal.

DAILY PRAYER EXERCISES

Day 2

SEEDS + SOIL

Warm-Up

Find a place where you won't be disturbed for about 15-20 minutes. Practice slowly breathing in and out to calm your body and quiet your thoughts. If today was a difficult day, try to release stress and anxiety with every exhaled breath.

Reading: Matthew 13:1-9

Seeds need good soil to grow. But Jesus knew that our hearts aren't always in the best condition to receive the seed of God's love. As you read the passage, try to picture the various types of soil Jesus describes.

> *That same day Jesus went out of the house and sat beside the sea. Such great crowds gathered around him that he got into a boat and sat there, while the whole crowd stood on the beach. And he told them many things in parables, saying: "Listen! A sower went out to sow. And as he sowed, some seeds fell on the path,*

and the birds came and ate them up. Other seeds fell on rocky ground, where they did not have much soil, and they sprang up quickly, since they had no depth of soil. But when the sun rose, they were scorched; and since they had no root, they withered away. Other seeds fell among thorns, and the thorns grew up and choked them. Other seeds fell on good soil and brought forth grain, some a hundredfold, some sixty, some thirty. Let anyone with ears listen!"

For Prayer & Reflection

1. Farmers understand that soil types are dependent on geography. Different patches of earth have different types of soil, which may or may not be beneficial for growing things. How would you describe the current condition of your heart? Is it hard? Rocky? Thorny? Fertile? What does the condition of your heart say about where you are on your journey with God?

2. **Read the parable again.** This time, instead of focusing on your "soil," ask God to show you his patch of earth. What do you see? What kinds of plants and trees grow in God's garden? What does this image say about the place that you're moving toward in prayer?

3. In your own words, tell God what you're thinking and feeling. If your "soil" doesn't seem very fertile, ask him to cultivate your heart and prepare it to receive the good seeds he is planting in your life.

4. Record your images and thoughts in your journal, along with anything else you are feeling about your relationship with God.

Day 3

A LOST SON

Warm-Up

Sit quietly for a few moments and rehearse the events of the day in your mind. As you consider each event or concern, let it drift out of your consciousness and fall out of your thoughts.

Reading: Luke 15:11-19

Every journey begins with a single step. As you read the story of the lost son, try to picture the scene in your mind.

> Then Jesus said, "There was a man who had two sons. The younger of them said to his father, 'Father, give me the share of the property that will belong to me.' So he divided his property between them. A few days later the younger son gathered all he had and traveled to a distant country, and there he squandered his property in dissolute living. When he had spent everything, a severe famine took place throughout that country, and

he began to be in need. So he went and hired himself out to one of the citizens of that country, who sent him to his fields to feed the pigs. He would gladly have filled himself with the pods that the pigs were eating; and no one gave him anything. But when he came to himself he said, 'How many of my father's hired hands have bread enough and to spare, but here I am dying of hunger! I will get up and go to my father, and I will say to him, "Father, I have sinned against heaven and before you; I am no longer worthy to be called your son; treat me like one of your hired hands."'

For Prayer & Reflection

1. The lost son realized that the only thing standing between him and his father was his own stubbornness. What arguments have you used to avoid a closer relationship with God? What are the real issues that your arguments represent? Ask God to speak to you about the attitudes and issues that are obstacles to a closer relationship with him.

2. *Read the parable again.* This time, try to focus on the son's reaction after he "came to his senses." Have you come to your senses yet? How do you feel? Guilty? Ashamed? Talk to God about what you're feeling, and ask him to give you the grace and strength you need for the journey ahead.

3. Spend a few more minutes in silence. Can you sense God's presence surrounding you? If you could describe what God's presence feels like in a single word, what would that word be?

4. As always, record your thoughts and anything you believe God is speaking to you in your journal.

Day 4

A STORM AT SEA

Warm-Up

As you prepare for your encounter with God today, recall the word you used to describe God's presence at the end of yesterday's prayer time. Let that word roll over and over in your mind until you return to the same sense of God's presence you had yesterday.

Reading: Matthew 14:22-33

Life is full of storms. As you read this passage about a storm at sea, try to picture yourself as a passenger in the disciples' boat.

> *Immediately he made the disciples get into the boat and go on ahead to the other side, while he dismissed the crowds. And after he had dismissed the crowds, he went up the mountain by himself to pray. When evening came, he was there alone, but by this time the boat, battered by the waves, was far from the land, for the*

wind was against them. And early in the morning he came walking toward them on the sea. But when the disciples saw him walking on the sea, they were terrified, saying, "It is a ghost!" And they cried out in fear. But immediately Jesus spoke to them and said, "Take heart, it is I; do not be afraid."

Peter answered him, "Lord, if it is you, command me to come to you on the water." He said, "Come." So Peter got out of the boat, started walking on the water, and came toward Jesus. But when he noticed the strong wind, he became frightened, and beginning to sink, he cried out, "Lord, save me!" Jesus immediately reached out his hand and caught him, saying to him, "You of little faith, why did you doubt?" When they got into the boat, the wind ceased. And those in the boat worshiped him, saying, "Truly you are the Son of God."

For Prayer & Reflection

1. Sailors depend on fair winds and calm seas to bring them back to port. When the wind turned against the disciples, it must have been scary, especially with night approaching. Have you recently experienced any rough weather in your life that has made you fearful or anxious?

2. *Read the passage again.* Try to picture yourself in Peter's shoes. Instead of Peter, Jesus is inviting you to leave the safety of the boat and walk on the waves. What happens next? Be honest. Does Jesus' presence help you walk above your waves of fear

and anxiety? Or do you feel yourself slowly sinking beneath the surface?

3. Talk with God about the things you're picturing and feeling. Ask him to unearth any lingering doubts you have about him and his willingness to carry you through the difficulties you are facing.

4. Journal about what happened when Jesus invited you to walk on the waves and record any comforting words God spoke to you today.

Day 5

THE CHILD

Warm-Up

Find a quiet place where you can experience a few minutes of solitude. If yesterday's "one word" exercise was helpful, do it again today. If not, use one of the other warm-up exercises you have learned.

Exercise

1. Imagine you are in a favorite place from your childhood, a place where you felt safe and at peace. A place that felt like home. Ask God to bring to mind an image of yourself as a child and picture this child seated across from you in this place. What do you say to the child? What does the child say to the "you" that exists today? How are you the same? How are you different?

2. Now imagine that Jesus enters the scene. Quietly observe how Jesus and the child version of you interact. What do they say to each another? Are

they talking at all or are they doing something else?

3. As the child fades from the scene, you find yourself sitting alone with Jesus. What does Jesus say or do? What do you say or do? Stay here as long as you like, telling Jesus whatever is on your mind.

Reflection

As your time with Jesus draws to a close, reflect on your experience.

- What age was the child you imagined at the beginning of the exercise?

- Why would God choose to show you the child you were at that age? Why was that age significant to you?

- Is there anything about your relationship with God at that age that you would like to recapture in your relationship with God today?

Record your thoughts and the things God showed you today in your journal.

Day 6

THE YOKE

Warm-Up

With your eyes closed, try to clear your mind and prepare your heart for time with God. When to-do list items or worries come up, acknowledge them and let them flow through your thoughts until they are completely out of your mind.

Reading: Matthew 11:28-30

Jesus valued periods of rest and relaxation. As you read his words, let them settle into the deep parts of your being.

> *"Come to me, all you that are weary and are carrying heavy burdens, and I will give you rest. Take my yoke upon you, and learn from me; for I am gentle and humble in heart, and you will find rest for your souls. For my yoke is easy, and my burden is light."*

For Prayer & Reflection

1. A yoke is a heavy, wood crosspiece that is bound to the necks of two oxen. Over time, the weight of the yoke can become burdensome, even for the strongest animals. Are you feeling tired and worn out? What is the yoke or burden that you have been carrying?

2. Although the yoke is attached to a plow or a cart, its primary purpose is to keep the oxen connected and pulling the load in the same direction. What or who is the other half of your yoke connected to? Are you pulling the load all by yourself? Are you pulling the load in different directions?

3. *Read the passage again.* Ask God to show you how the yoke Jesus describes is different from the one you have been wearing, and how your life might change if you were to wear his yoke instead of yours.

4. Spend a few minutes relaxing in God's presence. When the time is right, visualize yourself slipping free of the yoke you have been wearing and sliding into the yoke Jesus is offering you. Who or what is attached to the other side of the yoke now? Do you sense a difference in your attitude and outlook?

5. Record your thoughts and impressions in your journal. Your journal entry should include a description of how it felt to take off your yoke and take up Jesus' yoke.

Day 7

EMBER DAY #1

What is an "Ember Day?"

Today is an Ember Day. Since the fourth century, Christians have set aside periodic Ember Days as special times of prayer and personal reflection.

The term "Ember Day" derives from the Anglo-Saxon word, *ymb-ren*, meaning a circuit or revolution. In other words, an Ember Day isn't a one-time event, but a regularly occurring day for spiritual reflection and reconnection with God.

What you do on an Ember Day is entirely up to you. You can:

- Pray
- Read the Bible
- Spend time in nature
- Sit silently with God
- Engage in a hobby that nourishes your soul

On an Ember Day, you can do anything that helps you take a step back, slow down and hear what God is saying about your life.

Today's Focus

For the past week, you have been integrating moments of solitude into your busy life. Hopefully, your attempts to incorporate periods of prayer and solitude in your daily schedule have been fruitful.

But depending on your circumstances and responsibilities, it's possible that you have really struggled to find even a few moments for God each day.

Either way, today's Ember Day is a time to evaluate your progress and prepare for the week ahead.

Start by reviewing the strategies and techniques that have been effective in helping you become more aware of God's presence in your life.

- If you feel closer to God now than you did before you started your prayer journey, keep going—you're on the right track!

- If it's been difficult to maintain daily times of solitude, talk to God about shifting your priorities to make time for him in your schedule.

To gauge your progress on the journey into God, take a few minutes to review the thoughts and impressions you have written down in your journal. As you peruse your daily entries, look for themes to emerge about your concerns, anxieties and the movement of the Spirit during prayer.

Finally, talk with God about any obstacles or hurdles that are holding you back from sensing his presence in a deeper and more consistent way. These obstacles might include practical concerns like family or job demands, or they might be emotional barriers like fear, anxiety or distrust.

When your Ember Day is over, write down the prayer techniques and strategies that have increased your awareness of God's presence as well as anything else you believe God is trying to tell you today.

Day 8

THE LORD'S PRAYER

Warm-Up

Using one of the strategies and techniques for prayer and solitude that you identified during yesterday's Ember Day, go to your favorite prayer place and do the warm-up exercise that works best for you.

Prayer Focus

It's impossible to talk about prayer without eventually coming around to the prayer that Jesus gave his followers.

When the disciples asked Jesus how they should pray, he responded with something we now know as the Lord's Prayer (Matthew 6:9-13):

   a. *Our Father, who art in heaven, hallowed be thy name,*

   b. *Thy kingdom come, thy will be done, on earth as it is in heaven.*

c. *Give us this day our daily bread,*

d. *And forgive us our trespasses as we forgive those who trespass against us. Lead us not into temptation, but deliver us from evil,*

e. *For thine is the kingdom, and the power, and the glory, forever and ever. Amen.*

For Prayer & Reflection

- Pray the entire Lord's Prayer once or twice.

- Beginning with line (a), pray the Lord's Prayer one line at a time as follows:

    a. **Worship** God in your own words, telling him how important he is to you.

    b. **Ask** God to show you his thoughts and desires for you and for the people he has placed in your life. Then pray for God's "kingdom to come"—ask God to make his will a reality.

    c. **Thank** God for the gifts he has already given you and ask him for continued help in providing food, shelter and other necessities for your family.

    d. **Confess** your sins to God. Ask him to bring to mind any unforgiveness you may be harboring toward other people, then make a conscious decision to forgive them just as God has forgiven you.

e. **Listen** in silence for a few moments. Sit in God's presence, attentive for any words, thoughts or images he wants to communicate to you.

Conclude by praying through the entire Lord's Prayer one last time.

Day 9

THE HEALER

Warm-Up

Sit quietly for a few minutes and ask God to bring to mind a word or phrase to help you focus on him. Slowly repeat that word in your mind, gently pushing aside other thoughts and distractions.

Reading: Luke 7:20-23

God shows his unshakable love for us through actions as well as words. As you read the following passage from Luke's gospel, try to place yourself in the scene, and picture the sights and sounds of Jesus' ministry:

> *When (John's followers) had come to him, they said, "John the Baptist has sent us to you to ask, 'Are you the one who is to come, or are we to wait for another?'" Jesus had just then cured many people of diseases, plagues, and evil spirits, and had given sight to many who were blind. And he answered them, "Go and tell John what you have seen and heard: the blind receive*

their sight, the lame walk, the lepers are cleansed, the deaf hear, the dead are raised, the poor have good news brought to them. And blessed is anyone who takes no offense at me."

For Prayer & Reflection

1. When was the last time you noticed God in action? Has God ever demonstrated his love for you in a miraculous or unusual way? What impact did that event have on your faith and on your relationship with God?

2. *Read the passage again.* Ask God to bring to mind people you know who are sick, discouraged or in need. Now imagine placing each of these people in this passage. As they approach Jesus, he heals them and restores them to wholeness.

3. Return to the word God gave you during today's warm-up exercise. Ask God to show you why that word is so important today. Is he trying to tell you about an aspect of your life that needs healing or restoration?

4. Briefly journal about what God showed you today. Write down the word he gave you and why you believe it is important.

Day 10

A CLEAN SLATE

Warm-Up

If the word God gave you yesterday has meaning, return to it and repeat yesterday's warm-up exercise. If not, choose another warm-up exercise that is more helpful.

Reading: Psalm 51:1-17 (NLT)

Confession is good for the soul. During his darkest hour, David crafted a beautiful song of confession that is now found in Psalm 51.

As you read excerpts from his Psalm, let the words settle deep into your being. (If you prefer, feel free to read Psalm 51 in its entirety from your Bible.)

> *Have mercy on me, O God, because of your unfailing love. Because of your great compassion, blot out the stain of my sins. Wash me clean from my guilt. Purify me from my sin ... For I was born a sinner—from the*

moment my mother conceived me. But you desire honesty from the heart, so you can teach me to be wise in my inmost being. Purify me from my sins, and I will be clean; wash me, and I will be whiter than snow ... Restore to me again the joy of your salvation ... The sacrifice you want is a broken spirit. A broken and repentant heart, O God, you will not despise.

For Prayer & Reflection

1. God already knows your sins. But through confession, you have the opportunity to unload the burden of your sins and move forward with a clean slate. Ask God to bring to mind any specific sins that are holding you back from the life God wants you to live.

2. ***Read the passage again.*** This time, substitute the specific sins God showed you whenever you encounter the word "sin" in the Psalm. For example, instead of "Purify me from my sin," you could say, "Purify me from gossiping."

3. Take a few moments to reflect on your thoughts and feelings. Do you feel cleansed? Or do you feel guilty and ashamed? Talk to God about your feelings, especially if you feel condemned.

   You may also want to ask God if there are any acts of restitution you can do for sins that have affected other people.

Day 11

THE WOMAN AT THE WELL

Warm-Up

If the word God gave you on Day 9 continues to be meaningful, use it as your warm-up exercise for the entire week. Otherwise, try the empty cup/full cup exercise from Week 1.

Reading: John 4:23-26

When Jesus met the Samaritan woman at the well, the conversation quickly turned to the subject of worship. The Samaritan woman asked Jesus why the Jews worshipped in Jerusalem, while the Samaritans claimed a different place as the center for their worship. Jesus replied,

> *But the hour is coming, and is now here, when the true worshipers will worship the Father in spirit and truth, for the Father seeks such as these to worship him. God is spirit, and those who worship him must worship in*

spirit and truth." The woman said to him, "I know that Messiah is coming" (who is called Christ). "When he comes, he will proclaim all things to us." Jesus said to her, "I am he, the one who is speaking to you."

For Prayer & Reflection

1. What do you think Jesus means when he says that true worshipers will worship the Father in spirit and truth? Can you think of ways that worship (not just worship music) can become non-spiritual or untrue? What kind of worship is in your life?

2. *Read the passage again.* Now imagine you are alone with God in any setting you desire. Remind him of all the things he has done for you and the important role he plays in your life. If you can, eventually stop using words and simply pour out your soul to him in silence.

3. What is God saying to you now? Write down the highlights of your conversation with God in your journal.

Day 12

TEN LEPERS

Warm-Up

Today's prayer focuses on thankfulness. If you would rather not use a warm-up word to quiet your thoughts, gently reflect on the gifts God has given you.

Reading: Luke 17:11-19

Gratitude is a powerful spiritual resource. When Jesus encountered a group of lepers, he showed them how expressions of thankfulness can become remarkable acts of faith.

> *On the way to Jerusalem Jesus was going through the region between Samaria and Galilee. As he entered a village, ten lepers approached him. Keeping their distance, they called out, saying, "Jesus, Master, have mercy on us!" When he saw them, he said to them, "Go and show yourselves to the priests." And as they went, they were made clean. Then one of them, when*

he saw that he was healed, turned back, praising God with a loud voice. He prostrated himself at Jesus' feet and thanked him. And he was a Samaritan. Then Jesus asked, "Were not ten made clean? But the other nine, where are they? Was none of them found to return and give praise to God except this foreigner?" Then he said to him, "Get up and go on your way; your faith has made you well."

For Prayer & Reflection

1. Ask God to open your mind and imagine you are there with Jesus as he heals the lepers. What are some of the sights, sounds and smells you experience? How do the lepers react when Jesus heals them? Reflect on the way you reacted the last time you received a special gift from God.

2. *Read the passage again.* This time, imagine that you are accompanying the lone leper as he walks back to express his gratitude to Jesus. What is the healed leper saying or doing? How does he show his gratitude? Following the leper's example, take a few minutes to express your gratitude to God for the gifts and blessings he has given you.

3. *Read the passage one more time.* Jesus tells the thankful leper, "Get up and go on your way; your faith has made you well." What does that mean? Is Jesus talking about physical wellness, or is he talking about something else? Ask God to show you how gratitude has changed you and made you well.

4. Journal everything God revealed to you today, including the ways that God might be using gratitude to change you and "make you well."

Day 13

THE A.C.T.S PRAYER

Warm-Up

For today's warm-up, pick any exercise you have learned so far to center your thoughts on God's presence.

Exercise

The A.C.T.S. (Adoration, Confession, Thanksgiving, Supplication) prayer is a handy little prayer device that can be used when you are tired or don't have the energy to be very creative. It's also a helpful tool for maintaining balance in your conversations with God.

1. Beginning with *Adoration*, worship God in your own words. If you don't know where to begin, you could worship God using some of his many names (e.g., the Prince of Peace, the Alpha & Omega, etc.). Don't rush through the names, but pause over each of them for a few seconds before moving on.

2. Next, *Confess* your sins and shortcomings to God. Be honest, but don't go on and on, beating yourself up about every little failure in your life. Just admit what you've done wrong, receive God's mercy and move on.

3. After a few minutes of confession, transition to *Thanksgiving*. In addition to the everyday gifts God has given you, try to remember any special moments of God's goodness that you have experienced over the past few weeks. Express your gratitude in whatever way feels natural to you.

4. Finally, conclude your prayer with *Supplication* or "the wish list." It's okay to pray for your own wants and needs, but you should also leave time to intercede for the needs of others—friends and acquaintances, as well as the poor, the sick and the oppressed around the world.

Try to spend time on each of the four movements of the A.C.T.S. prayer. If God takes the conversation to a specific topic, follow his lead. But if he doesn't, try to spend as much time on Worship and Confession as you do on Thanksgiving and Supplication.

Day 14

EMBER DAY #2

Today's Focus

Believe it or not, you're halfway through your 30-day prayer journey.

At this point, you should feel more comfortable with prayer than you did a few weeks ago. You should also feel a little more aware of God's presence in your daily life.

On this Ember Day, reflect on your progress so far. Specifically, ask yourself (and God) the following questions:

- How has your relationship with God changed over the past several weeks?

- How effectively have you been able to use your imagination during conversations with God? What might be holding you back from a more imaginative prayer life?

- Has your daily prayer routine been consistent or sporadic? If consistency is a problem, what is preventing you from spending time in solitude? What adjustments do you need to make?

- Has your prayer life been boring lately? If *acedia* has set in, how do you plan to deal with it?

If you were unable to maintain a consistent prayer life this week, consider going back and praying any of the prayer exercises you missed.

Day 15

A SMALL VOICE

Warm-Up

Take a few moments to center yourself on God's presence using a warm-up technique of your own choosing. Since today's exercise is focused on hearing God's voice, ask God to speak to you during your prayer time.

Reading: 1 Kings 19:9,11-13

As you read the passage, try to imagine the sounds Elijah experienced as the Lord passed by.

> *Then the word of the Lord came to (Elijah), saying, "What are you doing here, Elijah?" ... He said, "Go out and stand on the mountain before the Lord, for the Lord is about to pass by." Now there was a great wind, so strong that it was splitting mountains and breaking rocks in pieces before the Lord, but the Lord was not in the wind; and after the wind an earthquake, but the*

Lord was not in the earthquake; and after the earthquake a fire, but the Lord was not in the fire; and after the fire (a still small voice). When Elijah heard it, he wrapped his face in his mantle and went out and stood at the entrance of the cave.

For Prayer & Reflection

1. Imagine that the Lord is approaching you the same way he approached Elijah. But instead of asking you to stand on the mountain, he is asking you to stand in the midst of the controlled chaos that is your everyday life. What do you hear? What are the typical noises that make it difficult to hear God's voice?

2. *Read the passage again.* This time focus on each noise, one by one, and imagine them fading into the distance. As the last noise fades away, what do you hear? Does God seem to be leading your thoughts in a certain direction? What thoughts, impressions or images come to mind?

3. Reflect on the things God may be saying to you. When Elijah heard God's still small voice, it prompted him to leave the security of his cave. Is the still small voice of God prompting you to do something today? How will you respond to it?

4. Take a few moments to journal about the thoughts, images or impressions that God used to speak with you today.

Day 16

THE PARTY

Warm-Up

Today's prayer exercise doesn't involve Scripture, so you might want to select a short Psalm to clear your mind of distractions and center your attention on God. Conclude your warm-up by asking Jesus to be present during your prayer.

Exercise

Imagination and intuition work together in prayer. One way to initiate a dialogue with God is to ask him to speak to you through a creative scenario.

- Picture yourself entering a ballroom filled with people. As you meander through the room, you recognize all of the guests. They are the people with whom you share important relationships—friends, family members, coworkers, etc. As you greet each guest, thank God for making him/her a part of your life.

- Now picture Jesus walking through the ballroom with you. You are the only one who notices his presence—he's invisible to everyone except you. As you go from guest to guest, ask Jesus to talk to you about your relationship with that person and let him show you the person's needs or challenges.

- Next, ask Jesus to point out a special guest, the guest who needs your help or prayers the most. Then, ask Jesus to tell you how to pray for this person. If there are several guests who need your prayers, try to get a sense about which person needs your prayers most urgently right now.

- Finally, take a few moments to pray for the special guest Jesus pointed out to you, and anything else Jesus showed you during your time together.

For Reflection

1. Were you surprised by some of the people who attended your party? Were you surprised by some of the people who didn't attend your party? What is God telling you about the relationships in your life?

2. Did Jesus give you any new insights about the people in your life? Or did he just confirm things you already knew? What did he show you about your special guest?

3. Record in your journal the name of the special guest and any insights Jesus revealed to you during today's prayer.

Day 17

WHO DO YOU SAY I AM?

Warm-Up

As you prepare for today's prayer, quickly jot down your to-do list on a piece of scrap paper. When you're finished, fold up the list and tuck it away in your purse or pocket. Then decide to give God your full attention for the next 15-20 minutes and set aside your to-do items until your prayer is finished.

Reading: Mark 8:27-29

As you read today's passage, visualize yourself somewhere in the scene Mark describes.

> *Jesus went on with his disciples to the villages of Caesarea Philippi; and on the way he asked his disciples, "Who do people say that I am?" And they answered him, "John the Baptist; and others, Elijah; and still others, one of the prophets." He asked them, "But who do you say that I am?" Peter answered him, "You are*

the Messiah." And he sternly ordered them not to tell anyone about him.

For Prayer & Reflection

1. Where are you in the scene? Are you among the disciples? Are you a fellow traveler? Or are you someone else?

2. **Read the passage again.** This time, imagine that Jesus turns to you and asks, "Who do you say I am?" How do you answer?

3. Now ask Jesus to show you who he is. Ask him to show you who he has been in your life up to this point, who he is in your life right now and who he will be as you move into the future.

4. When Jesus is finished speaking to you, return to praying for the special guest he pointed out to you during yesterday's prayer time. Be open to praying for this person in whatever way Jesus directs you.

Day 18

THE DECISION-MAKER

Warm-Up

Once again, today's prayer doesn't involve Scripture, so you may want to read a short Psalm to quiet your thoughts. When you're finished, ask God to be present during your prayer.

Exercise

Hearing God's voice is never more important than when we are wrestling with an important decision. When a decision looms on the horizon, here is a creative way to involve God in the decision-making process.

- Consider an important decision you need to make in the near future. Take a few minutes to reflect on the nature of the decision and how you have arrived at this point in your life.

- Make a mental list of all of the available options or possibilities.

- Now imagine that you have chosen the first possibility and it is three years in the future. Ask God to show you how your decision has affected your life and the lives of the people around you. Picture yourself explaining to God why you chose this option. Do you feel at peace? Or does your explanation make you feel unsettled?

- Repeat the previous step for all of the possibilities on your list. Pay careful attention to the way you feel when you explain to God why you chose each option.

- After you have worked through all of the possibilities, determine which one left you feeling most at peace and which one left you feeling most unsettled. The sense of peace you experience around a specific possibility will often be God's affirmation.

For Prayer & Reflection

1. Never base a major decision on the outcome of a single prayer session. In subsequent prayers, continue talking with God about your decision until you feel confident about the option you choose.

2. Before you end your prayer today, pray for the special guest from the Party Prayer on Day 16.

Day 19

LOVING ENEMIES

Warm-Up

Select a warm-up exercise to quiet your thoughts as you prepare to listen for God's voice today.

Reading: Matthew 5:43-48

> "You have heard that it was said, 'You shall love your neighbor and hate your enemy.' But I say to you, Love your enemies and pray for those who persecute you, so that you may be children of your Father in heaven; for he makes his sun rise on the evil and on the good, and sends rain on the righteous and on the unrighteous. For if you love those who love you, what reward do you have? Do not even the tax collectors do the same? And if you greet only your brothers and sisters, what more are you doing than others? Do not even the Gentiles do the same? Be perfect, therefore, as your heavenly Father is perfect."

For Prayer & Reflection

1. Pray through today's reading using the four stages of *Lectio Divina*: *Reading, Meditation, Response* and *Contemplation*.

2. What is God saying to you through this passage? Does today's reading relate to something you have been feeling about a person in your life? Does it shine a light on any steps or actions you need to take?

3. When you have finished praying through the passage, pray for your special guest from the Party Prayer again. What has God been saying to you about your special guest or your relationship with this person? Do you find yourself praying for this person at other times throughout the day?

Day 20

THE WORRY LIST

Warm-Up

In previous warm-up exercises, you tried to deliberately clear your mind of distractions so you could focus on God's presence.

For today's warm-up exercise, you are going to do the exact opposite. Instead of pushing worries, problems and concerns out of your thoughts, invite them into your awareness and write them down on a piece of paper.

Exercise

- Temporarily set aside your list of distractions and try to sense God's presence surrounding you at this very moment.

- Returning to your list, work down through your worries and concerns one by one, asking God to speak to you about each item.

- When you have finished working through the list, fold it and surrender it completely to God.

For Prayer & Reflection

1. Did God provide any insights about the worries on your list? Do you feel less anxious about your problems and concerns now that you have surrendered them to God?

2. Record in your journal what God said to you about each worry on the list. In the future, when you feel discouragement start to creep in, return to today's journal entry for encouragement.

3. Pray for your special guest from the Party Prayer one last time.

Day 21

EMBER DAY #3

Today's Focus

For the past six days, your prayers have centered on hearing God. Today's Ember Day focuses on evaluating your progress and discerning what God has said to you throughout the week.

- Have you found it easy or difficult to hear God's voice this week?

- Are you comfortable trusting your intuition in prayer? If not, what's holding you back?

- Are there any major themes that have emerged from this week's prayer exercises? Has God consistently spoken the same messages to you?

- Have you taken any steps to discern "divine diamonds from daydreams?" If not, today might be the perfect opportunity to review your journal and begin the discernment process.

This week you have also been praying for a special guest Jesus pointed out in the Party Prayer on Day 16.

- What has God shown you about this person?

- How has God directed you to pray for this person?

If it feels appropriate, reach out to your special guest today. You might want to tell your guest that you have been praying for him/her and offer words of encouragement.

If your relationship with this person has been damaged, take steps to mend the relationship or ask them for forgiveness.

Day 22

BREAD OF LIFE

Warm-Up

Find a comfortable, quiet place where you won't be disturbed for about 20 minutes. Begin your prayer by asking God to help you feel his presence in a special way. With your eyes closed, focus on your breathing and the peacefulness of the silence that surrounds you.

Reading: John 6:32-35

Contemplative prayer is one of the ways that God provides spiritual nourishment to his people. As you read the passage, pay attention to words or phrases that stand out to you.

> Then Jesus said to them, "Very truly, I tell you, it was not Moses who gave you the bread from heaven, but it is my Father who gives you the true bread from heaven. For the bread of God is that which comes down

from heaven and gives life to the world." They said to him, "Sir, give us this bread always." Jesus said to them, "I am the bread of life. Whoever comes to me will never be hungry, and whoever believes in me will never be thirsty.

For Prayer & Reflection

1. What words or phrases jumped out at you during the reading? What is God trying to tell you through those words or phrases? Spend a few minutes talking with God about the reading, and any other thoughts or emotions that are on your mind.

2. *Read the passage again.* Then slowly begin to center your thoughts on the word or phrase that emerged in the first reading. If no words or phrases came to mind, return to a word or phrase that has meaning for you.

3. Over the next several minutes, your mind should become increasingly free of distractions. As this happens, try to sense what the Spirit is doing, but don't overanalyze the experience. If a distraction enters your mind, return to your centering word until it fades out of your consciousness.

4. Stay in this place for several minutes, enjoying the stillness and basking in the warmth of God's presence. Resist the urge to make conversation with God. Instead, let him minister to your soul in the silence.

5. As your prayer comes to a close, reflect on the experience. What did you feel? Could you sense God's presence surrounding you? Was this different from what you have experienced before? How?

6. Record your thoughts and impressions in your journal.

Day 23

A CONTEMPLATIVE PSALM

Warm-Up

Begin today's prayer by recalling what you felt and experienced during yesterday's prayer. Talk to God about what you experienced and ask him to be with you again today.

Exercise

- The Psalmist tells us that praise and worship are gateways to the presence of the Lord (Psalm 100:4). Take a few moments to remember a Psalm that is special to you. If you can't think of a Psalm, thumb through your Bible and choose a Psalm or part of a Psalm that catches your eye.

- Once you have settled on a Psalm, read it several times and let key words of the passage roll over and over in your mind.

- With these key words drifting through your thoughts, imagine that you are sinking deeper into silence, stillness and God's embrace.

- Gradually let the words of the Psalm fade out of your consciousness as you become more aware of God's presence. The Psalm has done its job by bringing you through God's "gates" and into his "court." All that's left now is to enjoy a wordless encounter with God.

For Reflection

1. What was your Psalm? Can you think of any reason why you might have chosen this Psalm? Was this Psalm significant to you during a difficult part of your life?

2. For the rest of the day, occasionally allow your mind to return to your Psalm. At the end of the day, record the Psalm in your journal as well as anything God spoke to you through this Psalm throughout the day.

Day 24

THE TRAVELER

Warm-Up

To prepare for prayer today, return to yesterday's Psalm. Let the words soak into your soul like water saturating a dry sponge.

Reading: Luke 11:9-10

> *"So I say to you, Ask, and it will be given you; search, and you will find; knock, and the door will be opened for you. For everyone who asks receives, and everyone who searches finds, and for everyone who knocks, the door will be opened."*

For Prayer & Reflection

1. As you read the passage, imagine that you're on a journey. After traveling for days in the cold and rain, you see a cottage along the side of the road. The sun has set and the lights of the cottage call out to you in the darkness.

- *What emotions do you feel? Do any of these emotions reflect how you actually feel at this moment in your life?*

2. As you approach the cottage, you encounter a heavy, wood door. Before you knock on the door, you take a moment to think about what you will say to the cottage owner when he opens the door.

    - *What will you say to the cottage owner? Will you tell him about your journey? Can you tell him about the greatest need in your life right now?*

3. The door opens and you enter the cottage. Inside, it's warm and dry and filled with light. For the next few minutes, you do nothing but soak in your surroundings. All of the struggles you experienced on your journey are forgotten as you enjoy the moment.

    - *Stay in this place for a few minutes and give God access to the deepest parts of your being.*

4. You spent the entire night in the cottage. Outside, it's a new day. The clouds have disappeared and sunlight streams through the trees of the forest as you continue your journey.

    - *As your prayer comes to an end, what are you feeling?*

- *Do you have a sense that God has met or is meeting a need in your life?*

- *Has today's encounter with God changed you? If so, how?*

Day 25

THE A.C.T.S PRAYER REVISITED

Warm-Up

Reflect on yesterday's prayer. Have you noticed anything different? Has God continued to meet your needs today? How has your outlook changed, if at all?

After you spend a few minutes in reflection, prepare for today's prayer with a warm-up exercise.

Exercise

On Day 13, you prayed the A.C.T.S. (Adoration, Confession, Thanksgiving, Supplication) prayer. Today, we're going to revisit this prayer and add a contemplative twist.

- Pray the A.C.T.S. prayer the same way as before. If you need a refresher, refer to Day 13 of the Prayer Guide.

- As you pray the A.C.T.S. prayer, linger over any topics or areas where the Spirit seems to be drawing your attention.

- After you have finished the A.C.T.S. prayer, return to a centering word or phrase to refocus your thoughts and enter into a few moments of contemplative prayer.

- When you sense God is finished, gradually exit the stillness and reflect on today's encounter with God.

For Reflection

A lack of balance is an invitation to a self-absorbed prayer life. Contemplative prayer is great, but it has to be integrated into a routine that includes other types of prayer.

By combining the A.C.T.S. prayer with a contemplative element, you can restore balance when you feel you have been emphasizing one aspect of prayer more than others.

Day 26

THE BEATITUDES

Warm-Up

Select a warm-up exercise to quiet your thoughts as you prepare to listen for God's voice today.

Reading: Matthew 5:3-10

The Beatitudes contain rich nuggets for contemplative prayer. As you read the passage, try to listen to Jesus' words with your heart rather than your mind.

> *Blessed are the poor in spirit,*
> *For theirs is the kingdom of heaven.*
> *Blessed are those who mourn,*
> *For they will be comforted.*
> *Blessed are the meek,*
> *For they will inherit the earth.*
> *Blessed are those who hunger and thirst for righteousness,*
> *For they will be filled.*
> *Blessed are the merciful,*

*For they will receive mercy.
Blessed are the pure in heart,
For they will see God.
Blessed are the peacemakers,
For they will be called children of God.
Blessed are those who are persecuted for
righteousness' sake,
For theirs is the kingdom of heaven.*

For Prayer & Reflection

1. Pray through today's reading using the four stages of *Lectio Divina*: *Reading, Meditation, Response* and *Contemplation*.

2. When you reach the Contemplation stage, apply the things you have learned this week about contemplative prayer.

3. Has this week's understanding of contemplative prayer made the practice of *Lectio Divina* more rewarding than it was when you did it last week?

4. How has the introduction of contemplative prayer changed the way you approach familiar (and unfamiliar) Scripture passages?

Day 27

THE HITCHIKER

Warm-Up

Ask God to be present during today's prayer. Then use a centering word to focus your thoughts and clear your mind of distractions. Return to the centering word whenever a random thought disrupts your prayer.

Exercise

The Jesus-is-my-copilot concept isn't just a bumper sticker—it can also be useful as a starting point for contemplative prayer.

- Picture yourself behind the wheel of a car, driving down the highway. As the miles tick by, you notice that the roadside is littered with billboards depicting scenes from your life. The scenes are arranged in chronological order beginning with your childhood and leading up to the events you experienced earlier today.

- When the billboards reach the present moment, you pull over to the shoulder of the road to pick up a hitchhiker. The hitchhiker is Jesus. You move over to the passenger's seat and invite Jesus to take the wheel.

- With Jesus behind the wheel, you travel silently into your future. What do you see? What (if any) scenes do the billboards depict now?

- Eventually, you close your eyes and enjoy the ride. What does it feel like to be riding with Jesus? Do you feel safe? Are you tempted to open your eyes and look at the billboards again? Or do you keep your eyes closed?

For Reflection

1. When you were driving, how fast was the car going? What does that say about the pace of your life?

2. How fast was the car going when Jesus was driving? What does that say about the pace he wants to set for your life?

3. What was Jesus wearing? Does his clothing say anything about the role he currently plays in your life?

Day 28

EMBER DAY #4

Today's Focus

Today is the fourth and final Ember Day of your 30-day journey home to God. Like the previous Ember Days, today will shine a light on the progress you've made on your journey into God—your journey home.

In our experience, God often uses contemplative prayer to deal with personal issues you've been avoiding. Now that you've taken your first steps in contemplative prayer, it's possible that some of these issues have already started to emerge.

- How would describe your encounters with God this week?

- Has contemplative prayer led to a clearer sense of God's presence throughout the day? If so, make a mental note of the times and places you were most aware of his presence. If not, don't be discouraged.

As you move forward in prayer, God's presence will become more apparent to you.

- Did you suddenly feel the urge to cry this week? What were you doing or thinking when you felt this way? Although they can be uncomfortable, emotional responses are a sign that God is doing something significant in your life.

- At some point this week, did you suddenly remember a painful experience you thought was behind you? This may be a sign that you haven't fully dealt with the problem and God wants to bring healing to this part of your life.

Today is also the time to start thinking about where you will go from here.

- As your 30-day prayer journey draws to a close, do you have a plan to maintain prayer as a regular, daily exercise?

- Is God leading you to find a prayer partner or spiritual director to accompany you on your journey? If so, who will that person be?

Finally, take a few minutes to read through your journal entries for the past month and appreciate the progress you have made with God in just thirty days.

Day 29

THE LOST SON REVISITED

Warm-Up

Select a warm-up exercise to quiet your thoughts as you prepare to listen for God's voice.

Reading: Luke 15:11-20

On Day 3, your prayer focused on the story of the lost son—an appropriate metaphor for your journey home to God. As you read the rest of the parable today, be alert to any emotions or feelings that it stirs up in your mind.

> Then Jesus said, "There was a man who had two sons. The younger of them said to his father, 'Father, give me the share of the property that will belong to me.' So he divided his property between them. A few days later the younger son gathered all he had and traveled to a distant country, and there he squandered his property in dissolute living. When he had spent everything, a

severe famine took place throughout that country, and he began to be in need. So he went and hired himself out to one of the citizens of that country, who sent him to his fields to feed the pigs. He would gladly have filled himself with the pods that the pigs were eating; and no one gave him anything. But when he came to himself he said, 'How many of my father's hired hands have bread enough and to spare, but here I am dying of hunger! I will get up and go to my father, and I will say to him, "Father, I have sinned against heaven and before you; I am no longer worthy to be called your son; treat me like one of your hired hands."' So he set off and went to his father. But while he was still far off, his father saw him and was filled with compassion; he ran and put his arms around him and kissed him.

For Prayer & Reflection

1. How far away from God did you feel when you began your 30-day prayer journey? How far away from God do you feel today? What changed? Talk to God about the changes you have observed and ask him to show you the changes he has seen in your life.

2. The father met the lost son when the young man was still a long way from home. Although you may still feel a long way from home, you aren't traveling alone. The Father's presence is with you every step of the way. Spend some time praying contemplatively, sitting in the stillness of God's presence without an agenda.

3. When the father found his lost son, the celebration began. Conclude your prayer by celebrating your progress with the Lord and expressing your gratitude for what he is doing in your life.

Day 30

THE FIRST DAY (OF THE REST OF YOUR LIFE)

Today marks the beginning of a new chapter in your spiritual life. Starting today, the responsibility for structuring your daily prayers falls on your shoulders. The good news is that you now have several tools and prayer options to choose from:

Option #1: Repeat a Previous Prayer Exercise

Over the past thirty days, you have participated in twenty-nine different prayer exercises. If you're stuck and don't how to start your prayer, revisit one of the previous exercises. All of the prayer exercises in this book can be repeated—and God will probably show you new things every time you pray them.

Option #2: Lectio Divina

Lectio Divina is a wonderful tool for structuring your prayer. Starting with just a short passage of Scripture, you can quickly move into a rich conversation with

God that culminates in a period of contemplation—spiritual "fuel" for the journey.

Option #3: The A.C.T.S. Prayer

When time is limited, the A.C.T.S. prayer is a great way to start a conversation with God across a variety of topics. The simple A.C.T.S. acronym of Adoration, Confession, Thanksgiving and Supplication also makes a convenient prayer tool when you're driving, traveling or don't have access to a Bible.

Option #4: Your Own Creative Prayer Exercise

The past thirty days have taught you that creativity and intuition are God-given gifts that can be used in prayer. Use your creativity to design daily prayer exercises that are stimulating and exciting. Maybe you could even get together with a friend once or twice a week, and take turns sharing creative prayer exercises.

Option #5: Journaling

Hopefully, journaling has become an important part of your prayer routine. If you find it difficult to pray on a given day, pick up your journal and write down what you feel. In many cases, words on paper will develop into a full-blown conversation with God.

Option #6: Ember Days

Every now and then, it's helpful to schedule an Ember Day—a day to reflect on your spiritual progress.

What you do on an Ember Day is entirely up to you, as long as it helps you connect with God and leads to a time of spiritual self-assessment.

ABOUT THE AUTHORS

TIM MORRAL and **MELISSA McDONALD MORRAL** are authors and speakers with more than forty years combined teaching experience on topics related to the practice of Christian spirituality.

Tim holds a Doctor of Ministry and Melissa holds a Master of Divinity from Colgate Rochester Crozer Divinity School in Rochester, New York.

Together, they have served as writers, pastors, religious educators, workshop facilitators and nonprofit leaders.

Tim and Melissa regularly publish articles and other content about the integration of Christian practices with everyday life at www.GranolaSoul.com. They also lead workshops on prayer and practical spirituality for local churches.

For more information and resources, or to contact Tim and Melissa, visit their website at:

www.GranolaSoul.com

Made in the USA
Middletown, DE
21 December 2015